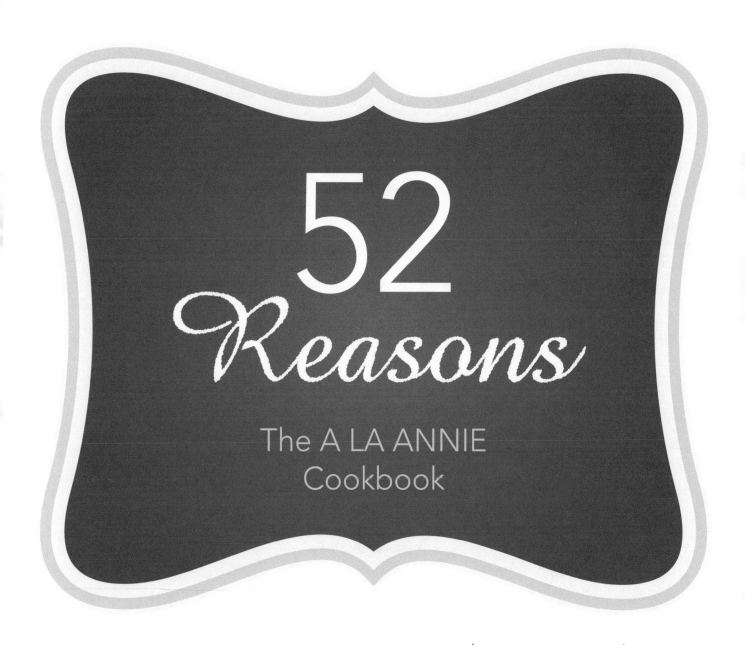

52
Reasons

The A LA ANNIE
Cookbook

Annie Rouleau-Scheriff (a la Annie)

Balboa Press books may be ordered through booksellers or by contacting:

Balboa Press
A Division of Hay House
1663 Liberty Drive
Bloomington, IN 47403
www.balboapress.com
1 (844) 682-1282

ISBN: 978-1-9822-5200-7 (sc)
ISBN: 978-1-9822-5201-4 (e)

Print information available on the last page.

Balboa Press rev. date: 11/18/2020

Recipe Acknowledgements:

Carol Chaundy, Antoinette Frontiera, Colette Hamel, Marguerite Rouleau, Claudine Manchester, Patty Miller, Theresa Mann, Helen McCoy, Wilma Zeleznik, Renee McBride, Maria Caton, Pat Cavannaugh, Bonnie Lynch, Lisa Gressens, Barbara Saros, Andree Abramoff, Jenn, Belinda and myself!

Saveur, Fine Cooking, At Home, Bon Appettit, Food and Wine, Gourmet, Louisiana Cookin', Good Food and countless other monthly food magazines that I turned to for inspiration.

Photo Acknowledgements:

Virginia O McCoy, Julie Caton, Mark Hamel, Jesse Rouleau, Christine Maccio and me!

Thank you to my husband Tony, my critic, Bonnie Lynch for the hundreds of culinary magazines she passed on to me, Carl & Virginia McCoy for years of support no matter what I was venturing into, my readers over those twenty years and to my very large family who all contributed in ways they will never know.

I would have never found my love for cooking without my dear friend Amy Breidenbach. Amy taught me how to cook at her parents beloved restaurant Cap's, Seaford Harbor, Long Island, New York.

Sadly, Cap's fell victim to the double punch of hurricanes Irene and Sandy. Even though the restaurant is gone it remains one of my great memories.

Lastly, 52 Reasons finally came together because my gal pal Amy Costello stepped up to the plate and helped this old lady bring this collection of recipes to light.

Table of Contents

Foreword

"One cannot think well, love well, sleep well if one has not dined well."
From <u>A Room of One's Own</u> published October 24, 1929
by Virginia Woolf, 1882 – 1941

My husband, Carl, and I met Annie in approximately the year 2000 while she was charismatically managing, hosting, tending bar, waitressing and whatever else needed doing at a local restaurant. We recognized her from her newspaper column photograph in which she wrote a weekly recipe.

We had followed her column for quite some time and asked her if she would be willing to cook for us. We were working long hours. She was!! She delivered meals for us several times a week leaving her creations in our refrigerator. It was magical to come home to see what was for dinner. We came to appreciate her recipes even more because we were sampling them. That led to saving clippings of our favorites that went into our folder marker "A la Annie."

When we had occasion to prepare something wonderful, we would consult our folder. We learned, early on in our relationship, that whenever Annie is, a party follows. This folder was a cookbook in the making. After we retired, I began photographing Annie's recipes as a way of serving to enhance her column. The idea of a cookbook was always on the horizon.

We watched and experienced Annie's cooking prowess developing over the years, her talent and artistry always having been evident. The book you hold in your hand is the culmination of years of hard work, experimentation and celebration.

Virginia O. McCoy
Grosse Pointe Woods and Glen Arbor, MI

"So perhaps the best thing to do is stop writing Introductions and get on with the book."
A.A. Milne, Winnie the Pooh

CHAPTER 1

THE FIRST

I couldn't believe it. The newspaper agreed to let me start doing a weekly
recipe column in the feature section. Like a panicked child I called my mom.
She said "start with my most requested ever recipe…. special jello".
The rest is *herstory.*

1 *Strawberry Ambrosia*

(This was my first ever recipe published in the paper.)

Ingredients

1 – 8oz. can crushed
pineapple with juice
2 small boxes strawberry
Jell-O
2 medium bananas, smashed
1 – 10oz. bag frozen
strawberries, chopped
2 cups boiling water
2 cups sour cream (1 pint)

Directions

In a large bowl, combine the Jell-O with the boiling water, crushed pineapple (with juice), strawberries and smashed bananas. Ladle half of the mixture into a glass 9 x 13 dish. Place in the refrigerator and chill for 2 hours. Leave the remaining mixture at room temperature.

Spread the sour cream (evenly) over the chilled layer, then carefully ladle the remaining Jell-O mixture over the sour cream. Chill for at least 2 hours before serving.

*The sour cream is a perfect complement to the sweet fruits that inspire this amazing ambrosia. This is my mother's recipe and a regular request at family parties for over 50 years!

EVERYTHING BUT THE BIRD, PIG, FISH OR COW

This was actually the name of a cooking class that was one of many that I instructed at the former Pointe Peddler on the Hill in Grosse Pointe Farms. The store invited local chefs to come and demonstrate recipes and techniques.

The next 8 recipes have become my absolute favorites to prepare and share whether at Thanksgiving, Christmas, New Year's or Easter.

The Bourbon Laced Cranberry recipe has made its way around the entire globe.

2 (Make Ahead) *Turkey Gravy*

Ingredients

3 lbs. turkey wings (or legs)
3 garlic heads, tops cut off, wrapped in foil
1 cup dry white wine
¾ cup chopped carrot
2 medium onions, peeled and quartered
8 cups chicken broth, divided
½ teaspoon dried thyme
¾ cup flour
2 tablespoons butter
½ teaspoon ground pepper

Directions

Preheat oven to 400°. Arrange the turkey wings in a large (greased) roasting pan and scatter with the onion. Roast at 400° for 1 hour 15 minutes, along with the foil wrapped garlic.

Transfer wings to a large (5 to 6 quart) pot. (Set aside the roasted garlic.) Deglaze the roasting pan with the wine, scraping the bits from the bottom of the pan. Add to the pot. Add 6 cups of the chicken broth to the pot, along with the carrots and the thyme. Bring to a boil, then lower to a simmer. Simmer, uncovered for 1 and ½ hours, stirring occasionally. Remove wings and discard. Strain the broth into a 3-quart sauce pan, pressing the vegetables to extract as much flavor as possible. Discard vegetables and skim fat from broth.

Whisk the flour into the 2 remaining cups of chicken broth. Bring the broth in the saucepan to a gentle boil. Stir in the broth/flour mixture and boil for 3 to 4 minutes. Squeeze the roasted garlic from the heads and whisk into the gravy along with the butter. Taste and season with additional salt and pepper as needed.

Transfer to containers and allow to cool. Store in refrigerator for up to 1 week or in the freezer for up to 6 months.

Reheat thawed gravy low and slow. I often stir in a smidgen of brandy just before serving!

If fresh herbs are your thing, tie up a small bunch of fresh thyme and throw it in the pot (instead of dried) before simmering.

3 Cranberries with Tawny Port Wine

Ingredients

1 – 12oz. bag cranberries
1 cup tawny port
1 ½ cups sugar
2 Tablespoons fresh lemon juice
1 teaspoon grated lemon rind

Directions

Combine all of the ingredients in a heavy pot. Bring the pot to a gentle boil then simmer until the berries begin to burst and the sauce begins to thicken, about 20 minutes or longer. (Use a wooden spoon to help the berries burst.)

Remove from heat and cool to room temperature. Transfer to an airtight container and refrigerate until ready to serve.

*These tasty cranberries soar beyond the turkey. Spread some on a peanut butter sandwich, a wheel of baked brie or even ice cream!

4 Bourbon Laced Cranberries

Ingredients

1 cup bourbon
¼ cup minced shallots
Grated zest of 1 orange
1 – 12oz. package cranberries
1 cup sugar
1 teaspoon fresh cracked black pepper

Directions

In a small saucepan, combine the bourbon, shallots, and orange zest. Bring the mixture to a boil over medium heat and simmer, stirring occasionally, until the bourbon is reduced to a syrupy glaze on the bottom of the pan, about 10 minutes.

Add the cranberries and the sugar, stirring well until the sugar dissolves. Reduce the heat lightly and simmer, uncovered, until most of the berries have burst open, about 10 minutes, or longer. (Use a wooden spoon to help the berries burst.)

Remove from heat and stir in the pepper. Transfer to a bowl and cool to room temperature. Store covered in the refrigerator.

*Bourbon is all the rage. This recipe has made its way all the way around the globe! Really!

5   *Spicy Sausage and Cornbread Stuffing*
(Homemade Cornbread)

Ingredients

1 stick butter (½ cup)
¼ cup olive oil
2 cups chopped onion
2 cups chopped celery
1 tablespoon finely chopped
fresh rosemary
1 lb. spicy (bulk) pork sausage
6 cups crumbled cornbread, store
bought or homemade*
1 cup chopped fresh parsley
¼ Madeira wine
Salt and pepper to taste

Directions

Melt the butter along with the olive oil in a large skillet over medium heat. Add the onion and the celery and cook and stir for 20 minutes or so, until the vegetables are very soft but not brown. Add the rosemary and season lightly with salt and pepper.

Transfer the mixture to a large bowl and set aside.

To the same skillet add the sausage and cook over medium heat, breaking up the sausage as it cooks, just until brown and cooked throughout.

Add the cooked sausage to the celery mixture along with the cornbread, parsley and Madeira. Toss well and season with additional salt and pepper to taste.

Preheat oven to 325 degrees. Transfer stuffing to a greased baking dish and bake at 325 for 30 to 40 minutes, until heated throughout and slightly golden on top.

*Prepare this flavorful stuffing a day or two in advance and store tightly covered in the refrigerator. Remove from refrigerator an hour or so before baking, to remove the chill.

*Homemade cornbread is recipe # 36

6 Bourbon Corn Pudding

Ingredients

3 large eggs
1 ⅛ cups evaporated milk
3 cups (2 -15oz. cans) cream style corn
3 cups frozen corn, thawed
3 tablespoons butter, melted
3 tablespoons brown sugar
3 tablespoons corn starch, dissolved in 3 tablespoons water
¾ teaspoon ground nutmeg
4 ½ tablespoons bourbon (optional)
½ teaspoon salt
½ teaspoon ground white pepper

Directions

Preheat oven to 350°. Coat 1 large (3 quart) or 2 smaller baking dishes with no-stick spray. Set aside. In a large mixing bowl, using an electric mixer, beat together the eggs and the evaporated milk. Stir, don't beat, in all of the remaining ingredients. Pour the batter into the prepared dish(es) and bake at 350° for 45 minutes or until a knife inserted in the center comes out clean. The top and edges of the pudding will be golden brown.

The size of the baking dish(es) doesn't really matter; however, the deeper the pudding, the longer it will take to bake. You can also bake the puddings in individual ramekins for a stepped up presentation.

*This corn lovers dream pudding is a snap to assemble. No chopping or dicing required! Choose a quality bourbon..

7 | *Sweet Potato Pie(s)*

Ingredients

3 lbs. sweet potatoes, peeled and cut into large chunks
1 package rolled pie crusts (2)*
(or from scratch, see below)
¾ cup packed brown sugar
3 eggs, beaten
1 – 12 oz. can evaperated milk
2 teaspoons pumpkin pie spice

For the glaze (optional)
1 stick butter
1 cup packed brown sugar
1 cup chopped walnuts or pecans, preferably toasted.

Directions

Heat a large pot of water to a boil. Add the sweet potato chunks and cook until tender, about 20 minutes or longer.

Meanwhile, fit the pie crust doughs into 2 greased pie dishes. Preheat oven to 375 degrees.

Drain and mash the potatoes. Stir in the brown sugar followed by the eggs, evaporated milk and the pumpkin pie spice.

Divide the mixture into the pie crusts. Bake at 375 for 35 to 40 minutes, depending on how deep the pie dish is. The filling in the crust should be set and pass the clean knife test.

While the pies are cooling, melt the butter in a small saucepan and whisk in the brown sugar. Pour the glaze over the pies and sprinkle with the chopped nuts.

*Skip the topping for a more savory pie that can served with the main course. Or cut the glaze in half and have one pie with the glaze and one without. Either way you end up with two great sweet potato pies. An extra for giving. Bonus!

*The super easy homemade pie crust, **recipe #30**, makes 2 crusts and is amazing.

8 *Fancy Holiday Peas*

Ingredients

1 -16 oz. package frozen peas, thawed
1 cup sliced fresh mushrooms
¼ cup chopped onions
2 tablespoons butter
1 teaspoon sugar
1 tablespoon chopped pimento
Salt and pepper to taste

Directions

Melt the butter in a medium skillet over medium heat. Add the mushrooms and the onion and cook until tender, about 7 minutes. Stir in the sugar, pimento and peas and cook and stir until the peas are thoroughly heated, about 7 minutes. Season with salt and pepper and serve.

I prepare my peas a day in advance. Before stirring in the peas, remove the skillet from the heat and cool mixture completely. Place the peas in an airtight bowl and top with the mushroom mixture. Toss well and store in the refrigerator overnight. Reheat the peas covered in a low (300°) oven, over medium heat on the stove top, stirring often, or even in the microwave oven. Toss after the first few minutes of cooking.

*Sometimes I toss in chopped, cooked bacon and substitute the pimento with chopped, sautéed peppers. Yum! Don't forget to season with salt and pepper!

9 Traditional Bread Stuffing with Sage

Ingredients

8 cups cubed STALE bread, cut into 1 inch cubes
3 eggs
2 cups chicken broth
½ cup whole milk
½ stick of butter
2 tablespoons olive oil
1 cup diced onion
1 cup diced celery
⅓ cup chopped FRESH parsley
3 tablespoons fresh chopped sage or 1 tablespoon dried
½ teaspoon each salt and pepper

Directions

Place the cubed, stale bread in a large bowl and set aside.

Melt the butter along with the olive oil in a medium skillet over medium heat. Add the onion and the celery and cook for 10 minutes or so, stirring often. The vegetables should be soft and translucent, just beginning to brown.

Preheat oven to 350 degrees.

While the vegetables are cooking whisk together 3 large eggs (4 if smaller) with the broth and the milk. Pour the mixture over the bread and allow to soak for a few minutes.

Add the cooked vegetables to the bread mixture along with the sage, parsley, salt and pepper. Toss gently until well combined. Taste and season with additional salt, pepper or sage to your liking.

Turn the mixture into a greased 8 X 10 rectangle bake dish.

Bake at 350° for 45+ minutes, until heated throughout and slightly browned.

This is a great stuffing choice for inside the bird. If the bread is not sufficiently stale, the mixture will be mushy.

SOUPS ON!

Soup has become a ritual in my little kitchen. Extra large pots are a familiar sight on my stove top. Boiling bones (chicken or ham), lots of chopped veggies and just the right seasoning will yield you a heaping pot of goodness. Some for now, enough for later and some more for the freezer.

If you have never made soup before I'm going to suggest that you start with the pasta a fagioli. It's straight forward and doesn't involve too mush prep. And it's delicious.

10 Pasta a Fagioli

Ingredients

½ cup extra virgin olive oil
2 cups chopped onion
3 tablespoons chopped garlic
1 cup chopped fresh parsley
(packed)
4 - 15oz. cans northern beans
(with juice)
2 - 15oz. cans vegetable or
chicken broth
1 - 15 oz. can diced tomatoes
(with juice)
1 cup dried ditalini pasta or other
small shaped pasta
grated pecorino Romano OR
Parmesan cheese for serving
Salt and pepper to taste

Directions

Heat the olive oil in a large, heavy pot over medium heat. Add the onions and cook for 10 minutes or so. Add the garlic and the parsley and continue to cook for a few minutes. Add the beans, vegetable broth and the tomatoes and bring the mixture to a boil, stirring often. Lower the heat to a simmer and stir in the pasta. Cover and simmer for 20 minutes or longer. Stir often.

Taste and season with salt and fresh pepper.

Ladle this simple, yet flavorful soup into bowls and garnish with grated pecorino Romano or Parmesan cheese and serve with crusty bread or crackers.

You'll want to freeze some of this good-for-you soup for another time. When reheating, you may want to add vegetable broth if the soup has thickened.

*If you have other fresh herbs (such as basil)
on hand, go ahead and stir them in!*

11 Rotisserie Chicken Noodle Soup

Ahhhh.....chicken noodle soup. There is nothing quite like it when you have a cold. Or when it is cold. The following is my favorite go to chicken noodle soup recipe. It begins with a warehouse rotisserie chicken (cooked) and finished with fresh vegetables and your noodle of choice.

Ingredients

1 - large cooked rotisserie chicken (or 2 smaller)
2 cups chopped celery
2 cups chopped carrot
2 cups chopped onion
4 to 5 garlic cloves, minced
1 to 2 tablespoons (or more to taste) Better than Broth, chicken flavor (or 4 to 6 bouillon cubes)
1 cup chopped fresh parsley
half package egg noodles (or your choice)

Directions

Begin by removing as much chicken from the bone as possible, both white and dark meat. Use your hands to shred the meat, then set side.

Place all of the bones in an 8 quart pot and fill the pot with water. Bring the pot to a boil, reduce to a simmer and cook for about an hour. Use a large, slotted spoon to remove all of the bones. Add more water if needed to fill the pot.

Add the celery, carrots, onion, and garlic to the pot. Simmer for another 20 minutes or so. Taste the broth and add some of the chicken base. Add the shredded chicken and the parsley. Taste and season with more chicken base if needed.

Add the noodles and simmer for another 10 to 15 minutes. Do a final check and season with salt and pepper to taste.

*This easy to prepare chicken noodle soup is perfect for first time soup makers. It's economical, makes a great freezer mate and it tastes way better than the stuff from a can.

12 *Easy, Delicious Vegetable Soup*

Ingredients

¼ cup olive oil
2 cups chopped onion
2 cups chopped celery
2 cups chopped carrot (peeled)
1 cup chopped fresh green beans
(about ¼ lb.)
1 large zucchini, chopped
1 bag shredded coleslaw
4 to 5 garlic cloves, finely
chopped
10 - 12 cups vegetable or chicken
broth
1 - 15oz. can diced tomatoes (with
juice)
1 - 6oz. can tomato paste
½ cup chopped fresh parsley
1 to 2 teaspoons dried basil
1 to 2 teaspoons dried oregano
Salt and pepper to taste
2 cans kidney beans, drained and
rinsed (optional)

Directions

Heat the olive oil in a large (heavy bottom) pot over medium heat. Add the onion, celery, carrot, and green beans and cook and stir for 10 minutes or so. Add the zucchini, coleslaw and garlic and cook and stir for another 10 minutes or so.

Add the broth, diced tomatoes, tomato paste, parsley, basil and oregano. Stir well and bring the pot to a boil, then immediately lower to a simmer. Cover and simmer for 30 minutes then taste for seasoning.

*Drizzle some over grilled Salmon or chicken. This flavor packed sauce (a little goes a long way) pairs perfectly with Roasted Brussels Sprouts and Kielbasa. Recipe # 22

S.O.S. (SAUCE ON THE SIDE)

Having spent the greater part of the last 40 years in the restaurant business, S.O.S. is the universal language when communicating to the kitchen that you would like the sauce to be served In the side.

These are my favorite (sauce) go to recipes. Is chutney really a sauce? Maybe not but you'll never want to serve it from a jar again.

13 Warm & Tangy Mustard Cream Sauce

Ingredients

½ cup heavy cream
¼ cup Dijon mustard
1 tablespoon honey
1 teaspoon apple cider vinegar

Directions

Combine all ingredients in a small sauce pan and bring to a simmer over medium heat. Cook for about 10 minutes. The sauce will slightly thicken.

This sauce pairs perfectly with Roasted Brussels Sprouts & kielbasa, recipe # 22

14

Amogue Sauce
(You're going to make this no-cook sauce again and again…)

Ingredients

1 large (28 oz.) can whole
tomatoes with juice
6 tablespoons extra virgin
olive oil
2 teaspoons dried oregano
6 to 8 large garlic cloves, coarsely
chopped
1 tablespoon lemon juice
Salt and pepper to taste

Directions

Use your hands to break apart the canned tomatoes into a medium bowl including the juice. Add the remaining ingredients and stir well to combine. That's it. Serve chilled or at room temperature. For optimum flavor make the sauce ahead of time and chill. This will give the flavors time to marry. Simply set the sauce out of the refrigerator for an hour or so before serving.

*Amogue sauce is a nice choice for steak from the grill. This versatile sauce is perfect for the warm weather because you don't have to serve it warm. You can heat it if you desire. Great on pasta or for Italian bread dipping. Yummy sauce!

15 *Honey Mustard Sauce*
(Made with 3 simple ingredients!)

Ingredients

1 cup mayonnaise
¼ cup yellow mustard (or your choice)
¼ cup honey
1 tablespoon finely chopped chives (optional)

Directions

Combine the mayonnaise, mustard and honey in a bowl and whisk until smooth. Refrigerate until ready to serve.

*Little ones will love this sweet and tangy dipper with chicken fingers or pretzel rods. Stir in some fresh (or dried) chopped chives, and this flavorful sauce is ready for the adult table.

16 *Michigan Chutney*
(You'll never buy the stuff in a jar again!)

Ingredients

1 tablespoon olive oil
1 large onion, halved and thinly sliced
2 large Granny Smith apples, peeled, cored, and chopped
⅓ cup maple syrup
⅓ cup apple-cider vinegar
7 oz. Michigan dried cherries (about a cup), or substitute jumbo raisons
½ teaspoon coarse sea salt
½ teaspoon black pepper
½ teaspoon dried thyme

Directions

Heat 1 tablespoon of olive oil in a medium skillet over medium high heat. Add the sliced onion and cook until the onion begins to soften, about 7 minutes. Add the chopped apple, syrup, vinegar and dried fruit. Cook the mixture, stirring often, until most of the liquid is absorbed, about 15 minutes. Remove from heat and stir in the salt, pepper and thyme.

Serve the chutney warm or at room temperature, alongside pork tenderloin or chops. *This delicious chutney is great sitting on a sharp cheese and charcuterie platter. Store leftover chutney in the refrigerator.

*Substitute with fresh thyme by tying a small bundle of sprigs together and adding it to the skillet from the very beginning of the recipe. Just remove it at the end.

Annie Rouleau-Scheriff (a la Annie)

Chilled Mustard Sauce

17

Ingredients

1 cup mayonnaise
¼ cup Dijon mustard
2 teaspoons fresh lemon juice
¼ teaspoon dried dill weed,
parsley or chives (optional)

Directions

Combine all ingredients and whisk until smooth. Store in refrigerator until ready to serve. Serve with just baked salmon cakes (**recipe # 32**) or smeared on chicken or a burger. This yummy sauce sits nicely on your favorite "Deli Style" sandwich.

*Serve with just baked salmon cakes. Recipe # 32 Or smear some on a burger or your favorite deli style sandwich.

BLAST FROM THE PAST

Whimpy's and JL Hudsons are no longer in existence but the memory of going to both of those places

I hope that the Maurice salad recipe will bring back a happy memory for you.

18

Whimpy Fries

(The bar might be gone but this recipe will live forever.)

Ingredients

1 – 20 oz. package Simply Potatoes (shredded for hash browns)
3 tablespoons olive oil, divided
Salt and pepper to taste
1 large onion, halved and thinly sliced
5 to 6 slices American cheese

Directions

Heat a 10 inch no-stick skillet over medium heat. Toss the shredded potato with 2 tablespoons of the olive oil, and the salt and pepper. Turn the potatoes into the hot skillet and press down. Cover and cook for 10 to 15 minutes, allowing the bottom of the potatoes to become dark brown and crisp. Flip the potatoes over and cook for another 10 to 15 minutes, covered.

Meanwhile, heat the remaining 1 tablespoon olive oil in a small skillet and add the onion. Cook the onion over medium heat until it becomes soft and translucent, about 10 minutes. Scatter the sautéed onion over the potatoes and top with slices of American cheese. Cover and continue to cook for a few more minutes, until the cheese is melted but not browned. Transfer to a serving platter, cut into wedges and serve.

*We used to love sitting at the bar on East Warren and watching Eric the cook/comedian in action over the hot griddle. It was like a free show with dinner!

19 J.L. Hudson Maurice Salad
(This recipe brings back memories of special lunches at Hudson's)

Ingredients

Maurice dressing
1 cup mayonnaise
1 tablespoon white vinegar
2 hard cooked eggs, quartered
½ cup chopped onion
1 teaspoon Worcestershire sauce
½ cup vegetable oil
1 large (or 3 small) sweet pickles, sliced
1 cup sour cream
1 teaspoon dried chives
½ teaspoon salt

Salad
1 head of iceberg, shredded (or 3 romaine hearts)
6 oz. Swiss cheese, halved and cut into match sticks
6 oz. thick sliced ham, halved and cut into match sticks
1 cup (or more) chopped (shredded) cooked white meat chicken
2 large (or 6 small) sweet pickles, cut into match sticks
6 extra large pimento stuffed olives, sliced

Directions

Maurice dressing

In a food processor (or blender) combine the mayonnaise with the vinegar, eggs, onion, Worcestershire sauce, oil and pickles.

Pulse several times until the mixture is smooth. Transfer to a medium bowl and whisk in the sour cream, chives and salt. Cover tightly and refrigerate until ready to serve.

Salad

In a large bowl toss the lettuce with the Swiss cheese, ham, chicken, pickles and olives. Pour about ¾ cup of the dressing over the salad mix and toss until the dressing is distributed evenly throughout the salad.

Garnish with sliced hard cooked egg, sliced pickles and fresh parsley. Serves about 4.

*It was always a special occasion at the Oakland Mall Hudson's restaurant overlooking the mall. They served a little hard roll as a side car on the salad plate.

The dressing will keep in the refrigerator for about a week. Smear some on a sandwich or dip a chip in it. Yummy.

20 Savannah Sin

Ingredients

1 – 1 to 1 ½ lb. whole loaf sourdough bread (or round), not sliced
2 cups shredded extra sharp cheddar cheese
1 – 8 oz. block cream cheese, softened
1 ½ cups sour cream
⅓ cup chopped scallion
1 – 4 oz. can green chilies
⅛ teaspoon Worcestershire sauce
1 cup chopped cooked ham

Directions

Preheat over to 350°. Using a serrated knife, cut the top off of the bread, just inside the edge. Save the top of the bread. Remove the center of the bread, leaving a thick shell to bake the dip in. Set aside.

In a food processor, combine all of the remaining ingredients except for the ham. Pulse several times, until the mixture becomes smooth, scraping down the sides of the bowl with a rubber spatula. Add the ham and give the processor just a few more pulses. Turn the dense into the bread shell and replace with the top of the bread. Securely wrap in foil, then bake (directly on the oven rack) for 2 hours.

Unwrap the loaf, remove the top and place on a serving platter. Spread the dip on crackers, party rye, pita bread, or even veggies. Cut the lid of the loaf into wedges and share the flavor.

When the dip is gone, cut the bread shell into flat pieces and place under the broiler until golden brown. Yummy. There's no sin in that.

*Don't waste anything. Dry out the bread that you pulled from inside the loaf and make some bread crumbs!

FAMILY MATTERS

Many of the recipes in this chapter have come from family. And friends. There were times when I used to think "what am I going to put in the paper next week?" As the years rolled on, people would come to me with a family favorite (recipe) of their own. These are the best of the best.

21 7 – Layer Salad

7 – Layer Salad has been a long time favorite of my family. My mother's take is a mixture of crunchy greens nestled under a thin blanket of mayonnaise, topped with shredded cheddar cheese. This, more than delicious salad, is prepared a day in advance making it a perfect choice when you're in charge of the meal. I usually make the salad in a 9 x 13 glass dish, but if you have a trifle bowl you can double up the layers for a stellar presentation.

Ingredients

1 package of three hearts of Romaine, chopped
1 ½ cups diced celery
⅔ cup finely chopped scallion
1 – 12 oz. package frozen peas
1 ½ cups mayonnaise
2 to 3 teaspoons sugar
2 cups shredded cheddar cheese

Directions

Place the chopped romaine in a glass 9 x 13 dish. Scatter the chopped celery over the lettuce, followed by the chopped scallions. Spread the frozen peas over the scallions. Using a spatula, carefully spread the mayonnaise evenly over the peas. Sprinkle the sugar over the mayonnaise, then scatter the shredded cheddar over the top. Cover securely with plastic wrap and store in the refrigerator overnight and until ready to serve.

*The mayonnaise layer becomes just the right amount of dressing in this salad that seems to toss itself as it's being served!

22 Roasted Brussels Sprouts with Kielbasa, Red Onion

Ingredients

1 lb. Brussels Sprouts, halved lengthwise
2 cups red onion, halved and cut into ½ inch wedges (about 1 large)
1 lb. kielbasa, cut into ½ inch slices
2 tablespoons olive oil
Salt and pepper to taste

Directions

Preheat oven to 450°. In a large bowl toss together the sprouts, onion, and kielbasa. Add the olive oil, 1 tablespoon at a time, drizzling over the vegetables/kielbasa and tossing well to coat evenly.

Season with salt and pepper. Toss and season again. Toss again and spread the mixture into a single layer on a baking sheet. Bake at 450° for 20 to 25 minutes, until the sprouts are tender, yet crisp. The sprouts, onions and kielbasa will be beginning to char just a little. (That charring brings out the sweet flavor of the vegetables.)

*A "carb" cutters choice for sure. Serve with warm and tangy mustard cream sauce "on the side" – recipe #13

Annie Rouleau-Scheriff (a la Annie)

23 Italian Turkey Meatloaf
(You won't miss the beef!)

Ingredients

2 lbs. ground turkey
1 – 6 oz. can tomato paste
½ cup chopped sun-dried
tomatoes (packed in oil)
1 tablespoon Worcestershire
sauce
1 cup panko (Japanese bread
crumbs), or other breadcrumbs
⅓ cup dried minced onion (or 1
cup finely minced fresh onion)
2 tablespoons dried parsley, plus
more for garnish (or ½ cup fresh)
4 eggs
1 teaspoon dried oregano
1 teaspoon dried basil
1 teaspoon EACH salt and
pepper
1 to 2 tablespoons <u>fresh</u> chopped
garlic (personal preference)
1 cup ketchup, for topping

Directions

Preheat oven to 350°. Grease a large glass baking dish (such as a 9 x 13) and set aside.

Place the ground turkey in an extra large bowl. To the turkey, add all of the ingredients, except the ketchup. Using clean hands, toss and mix the meat with the other ingredients until everything is very well blended. This process will take about 5 minutes. Turn the mixture into the prepared baking dish as evenly as possible. Spread the ketchup over the meat loaf. Sprinkle some parsley (dried or fresh) over the ketchup.

Bake the meatloaf at 350° for about an hour, until browned on the edges and cooked throughout. (A deeper baking dish may need a bit more time.)

*Have a cold turkey meatloaf sandwich with the leftovers. Yummy!

24 *Big Batch Marinara Sauce*

Ingredients

½ cup olive oil, divided
3 medium-large onions, diced
12 garlic cloves, minced (or more to taste)
1 tablespoon dried oregano
1 tablespoon dried basil
2 tablespoons dried parsley
3 bay leaves
1 – 105 oz. can whole tomatoes (or 4 x 28 oz.)
1 – 105 oz. can crushed tomatoes (or 4 x 28 oz.)
½ bottle dry red wine (about 1 ½ cups)
2 tablespoons sugar
4 inches of parmesan cheese rind

Directions

Heat ¼ cup of the olive oil over medium heat in a large, heavy stock pot. Add the onion and the garlic and cook and stir for 20 minutes or so, adding additional olive oil as the onions cook. The onions should be soft and translucent, not brown.

Meanwhile, in small batches, puree the whole canned tomatoes in a food processor or blender and set aside, with the juice from the can.

Add the oregano, basil, parsley and bay leaves. Cook and stir for a minute or two. Add the pureed tomatoes and crushed tomatoes to the pot, followed by the wine, sugar and parmesan cheese rind. Slowly bring the pot to a simmer, then lower the heat and cook for several hours (at least three), stirring often. You want to make sure that your sauce does not burn.

*Taste and adjust seasoning to your liking. Portion and freeze sauce for easy week night suppers.

25 BBQ Sloppy Joes

Ingredients

1 tablespoon olive oil
½ cup chopped onion
1 lb. lean ground beef (or ground turkey)
1 garlic clove, chopped
Salt and pepper to taste
¾ cup barbecue sauce (your choice)
½ cup ketchup
2 tablespoons brown sugar
2 teaspoons Worcestershire sauce
8 medium burger rolls

Directions

In a medium no-stick skillet, combine the oil, onion, beef, garlic, salt and pepper. Cook and stir over medium heat for 5 to 7 minutes, until the meat is brown and crumbled. Drain any visible fat. Add the barbecue sauce, ketchup, brown sugar, and Worcestershire sauce. Bring the mixture to a boil, then reduce to a simmer and cook and stir for about 15 minutes, uncovered. Cover the skillet and cook on low for another 10 minutes or so to allow the flavor of the meat to marry with the sauce. Ladle the meat onto toasted burger buns or into lettuce wrappers.

*The entire family will love the sweet and tangy sauce of "Wilma's" take on this American classic.

26   *Carrot Cake*

Ingredients

3 cups grated carrots
2 cups flour
2 cups sugar
1 tsp salt
2 tsp soda.
2 tsp cinnamon
4 eggs
1 ½ cups oil
1 cup nuts, chopped

Cream Cheese Frosting
8 oz. cream cheese, softened to room temperature
1 stick butter, softened to room temperature
3 cups confectioner's sugar
1 teaspoon vanilla

Directions

Mix all of the above. Pour batter into a greased 9 x 13 cake pan. Bake at 325-350° for about 50 minutes, depending on your oven temperature accuracy. Cool completely before frosting.

Cream Cheese Frosting

Cream together the cream cheese and the butter. Add the confectioner's sugar and the vanilla and beat until smooth. If the frosting is too thick add a bit of milk.

*My sister Colette has been treating my family to this over the top carrot cake for decades. Save time and effort by starting with already shredded carrots.

27 Slow Roasted Tomato Sauce

Ingredients

¼ cup extra virgin olive oil, plus 1 cup extra virgin olive oil (or less), divided
1 to 2 large onions, diced
10 garlic cloves or more to taste, peeled, smashed and coarsely chopped
2 to 2 ½ lbs. fresh garden tomatoes (any variety), chopped
½ cup fresh basil leaves, torn
1 teaspoon salt, plus more to taste
1 teaspoon sugar
¼ teaspoon red pepper flakes (optional)

Directions

Heat ¼ cup olive oil in a large, deep, over proof skillet over medium heat. Add the onions and the garlic and cook and stir until the onions become tender, about 10 minutes or more. Remove from heat and add the tomatoes, basil, salt, sugar and red pepper. Gently toss to combine. Add the remaining 1 cup oil. The olive oil should come about half way up the tomatoes. You may not need an entire cup of the oil.

Preheat oven to 250°. Place the skillet in the oven and slow roast for 3 hours, stirring occasionally.

Serve just from the oven tomatoes over cooked pasta or in small bowls with a side of crusty bread.

I freeze the tomato in 3 cup freezer safe containers. That seems to be just enough for a pound of pasta, perfect dinner surprise for when the weather turns chilly.

*Always thaw frozen tomatoes first, then reheat low and slow on the stove top.

*At the end of summer when tomatoes are bountiful I double the recipe.

28 Gratin of Zucchini, Summer Squash and Tomato

Ingredients

5 tablespoons olive oil, divided
2 medium onions, halved and thinly sliced
1 ¼ lbs. Roma (or other) tomatoes, sliced into ¼ inch slices
¾ lbs. each zucchini and summer squash (about 2 small), cut into ¼ inch thick slices
4 tablespoons fresh thyme leaves, divided
Salt and pepper to taste
1 ¼ cups grated parmesan, divided

*If you don't have fresh thyme on hand you can use dried, but cut the amount to 3 teaspoons. This recipe can easily be doubled.

Directions

Heat 2 tablespoons of the oil in a medium pan over medium heat. Add the onions and cook and stir until the onions become limp and golden, about 20 minutes. Lower the heat if the onions brown too quickly. Spread the cooked onions in the bottom of a 2 quart glass baking dish that has been coated with no-stick spray. Sprinkle with 1 tablespoon of the thyme leaves. Set aside.

Preheat the oven to 375°. In a medium bowl, toss the zucchini and squash with 1 ½ tablespoons of olive oil, 2 tablespoons of thyme leaves and season lightly with salt and pepper.

To assemble the gratin, start at one end of the prepared baking dish (with the onions and the thyme) and lay a row of slightly overlapping tomato slices. Sprinkle with a little (1 teaspoon or so) of the parmesan cheese. Next, lay a row of (slightly overlapping) zucchini slices alongside of the tomato row, overlapping the tomatoes by two-thirds. Sprinkle with more parmesan cheese. Follow next (using the same method) with a row of squash slices (overlapping the zucchini) and sprinkle with parmesan cheese. Repeat the entire process (tomato, zucchini, squash) until the dish is full. Drizzle the remaining olive oil over the gratin. Combine the remaining parmesan cheese with the remaining 1 tablespoon of thyme and sprinkle over the gratin. Bake at 375° for 65 to 70 minutes, until the juices have bubbled for a while and reduced considerably. Let cool for at least 15 minutes before serving.

29 Fresh Fettuccine A La Orange

Ingredients

1 – 9 oz. package fresh fettuccine
3 to 4 tablespoons olive oil
1 medium onion, halved and
thinly sliced
6 slices cooked bacon, cut into
bite sized pieces (not crumbled),
about 1 cup
2 teaspoons chopped fresh
rosemary
3 tablespoons orange marmalade
Salt and pepper
Parmesan cheese for serving

Directions

Bring a medium pot of water to a boil. Meanwhile, in a medium no-stick skillet heat 3 tablespoons of the olive oil over medium heat. Add the onion and cook until the onions begin to brown (not burn) about 10 minutes or so. Give the onions time to start browning before you stir them. Add the bacon and cook for a few more minutes. Add the rosemary and the marmalade and stir to combine. Taste and season with salt and pepper. Lower the heat to low.

Place the pasta in the boiling water and cook for 3 minutes or so. Drain the pasta, reserving ½ cup of the cooking water. Add the drained fettuccine to the skillet and toss with the marmalade mixture. Add ¼ cup of the reserved pasta water and continue to toss until well combined. Add more pasta water if needed. Serve immediately topped with grated parmesan cheese.

*Enjoy fettucine a la orange as a meal or paired with fresh salmon from the grille.

30 My Mom's Apple Pie (& Crust)

Ingredients

For the filling

6 to 8 tart apples, peel, cored and thinly sliced *My mother's choice is McIntosh apples
1 tablespoon lemon juice (optional)
¾ cup sugar, plus a bit more for dusting the top crust
2 tablespoons flour
⅔ teaspoon cinnamon
Dash or two of ground nutmeg
2 tablespoons cold butter, halved and quartered

For the crust (this recipe is AWESOME!!!!)
2 cups flour
⅔ cups vegetable oil
⅓ cups whole milk
Wax paper for rolling out the dough

Directions

Place the prepared apple slices in a large bowl. If the apples are on the sweeter side, toss with the lemon juice. In a small bowl, combine the sugar with 2 tablespoons flour, the cinnamon and the nutmeg. Sprinkle the mixture over the apples and toss well to evenly coat the apple slices. Set aside.

Preheat oven to 400°.

Place the 2 cups flour in a medium bowl. Whisk together the vegetable oil with the milk then add, all at once, to the flour. Mix well to form a ball of dough. (If the dough seems dry, add a few drops of milk.) Divide the dough into 2 pieces with one being ⅔ of the dough and the other being ⅓.

Wet a flat surface with a few sprinkles of water. Lay a sheet of wax paper over the surface. Place the larger half of the dough on the wax paper and cover with another sheet of wax paper.

Using a rolling pin, carefully roll out the dough (working from the edges first, not the center) to create a circle about 1 inch larger than your 9 or 10 inch pie plate. Remove the top sheet of wax paper then pick up the bottom sheet of wax paper and invert the dough into the pie plate. Fit the dough around the edges evenly. Spoon the prepared apples into the crust, along with any juices from the bottom of the bowl. The apples will be piled high but will cook down while baking. Dot the apples with the cubed butter.

Repeat the steps with the wax paper and roll out the smaller dough. Place the dough over the apples and carefully remove the wax paper. Use your fingers to pinch the bottom and top dough together around the edge of the pie.

Use a sharp knife to cut 3 – 4 inch slits in the top dough to allow steam to escape. Sprinkle the top of the dough with ½ teaspoon sugar.

Bake at 400° for 50 minutes to 1 hour, until slightly more than golden brown.

*My mom has been baking this pie (2 at a time) for over 50 years! Mother of nine. Mother of mine.

31 Macaroni and 4 Cheese

Ingredients

1 lb. elbow macaroni, shells or other bite-sized pasta, cooked to package directions
½ cup butter
1 ½ cups heavy cream, divided
1 – 1 lb. block Velveeta cheese, cut into large cubes
½ cup shredded cheddar cheese
½ cup shredded Monterey Jack cheese
½ cup grated Parmesan or Romano cheese (or a mix of both)
4 to 5 dashes of hot sauce (optional)

Directions

Preheat oven to 350°.

In a medium heavy saucepan, melt the butter, ½ cup of the heavy cream and the Velveeta cheese over low heat, stirring often. When the Velveeta has completely melted, stir in the Cheddar, Jack, Parmesan, another half cup of the heavy cream and the hot sauce. Gently stir to blend the cream with the melted cheese. Cook and stir over low heat until the cheese mixture becomes smooth and creamy.

Place the cooked, drained pasta in a large mixing bowl that has been coated with non-stick spray. Pour the cheese mixture over the noodles and toss and stir until all of the pasta is evenly coated. Turn the cheese noodles into a 8 x 10, or similar size baking dish that has been coated with non-stick spray. Cover with foil and bake at 350° for 25 to 30 minutes. Uncover and drizzle with the remaining ½ cup heavy cream.

Continue to bake (uncovered) for another 20 to 25 minutes, until bubbly and golden brown around the edges.

*This creamy cheesy mac and cheese will become a family favorite for sure.

32 *Sockeye Salmon Cakes with Chilled Mustard Sauce*

Ingredients

3 – 6 oz. cans sockeye salmon, drained and flaked (or other canned salmon)
⅓ cup chopped scallions
½ cup panko (Japanese bread crumbs)
2 eggs
½ cup mayonnaise
1 tablespoon Dijon mustard
2 teaspoons Worcestershire sauce
½ teaspoon salt
¼ teaspoon white pepper
1 tablespoon dried parsley
1 tablespoon olive oil

Directions

Place the flaked salmon in a medium bowl and toss with the scallions and the panko. Set aside. In a small bowl, whisk together the eggs with the mayonnaise. Whisk in the Dijon, Worcestershire sauce, salt, pepper and parsley.

Pour the mixture over the salmon and gently mix and toss until well combined. Refrigerate for at least one hour or up to overnight.

Preheat the broiler with the rack in the center of the over. Using a ⅓ cup as a measure, form the salmon mixture into 7 cakes or so, placed about 2 inches apart on a greased bake sheet. Use a spatula to gently mash down the cakes to form ½ inch thick cakes. Use a pastry brush to blot just a touch of olive oil on each cake.

Place in the oven under a hot broiler and cook until the cakes become a deep golden brown, 10 minutes or longer. Cooking time under a broiler varies considerably from oven to oven. Start checking on the cakes as soon as 8 minutes into the cooking time. Remember that cook time will vary depending on your broiler.

Serve with chilled Mustard Sauce (recipe #17) OR Warm and Tangy Mustard cream sauce (recipe #13)

33 Tailgate Burritos

Ingredients

2 lbs. boneless, skinless chicken breasts
1 – 12 oz. beer
1 chicken bouillon cube
1 tablespoon chopped garlic
1 cup sour cream
3 tablespoons Hidden Valley Ranch salad dressing and seasoning mix (1 – 1oz. packet)
2 cups shredded cheddar (or Mexican blend) cheese
8 or more – 8 inch soft flour tortillas

*Or bake in the oven or toaster oven, wrapped in foil for about 25 minutes at 350 degrees.

Directions

Place the chicken in a large deep sauté pan and add the beer, bouillon cube and garlic. Then add water just until the chicken is completely submerged in the liquid. Bring the liquid to a boil and poach the chicken over a medium simmer until cooked throughout, stirring occasionally. Make sure to check the thickest piece of chicken for doneness. The larger the chicken breasts, the longer the poaching time. Flip the chicken often so it doesn't get dried out.

Remove the chicken from the liquid and place in a large bowl (to cool for about 10 minutes.) Reserve the liquid. Using a knife and fork, cut (shred) the chicken into small pieces.

Pour a half cup (or so) of the reserved cooking liquid over the shredded chicken.

Stir the ranch mix into the sour cream, then toss with the chicken. Add the shredded cheese and toss well until everything is well incorporated.

Working with a few tortillas at a time, measure 1/2 cup of the chicken filling onto the lower middle of a tortilla. Form the mixture into a 3 inch log, then carefully roll the burrito, folding the ends in before completing the roll. Wrap each burrito in foil and store in the refrigerator until ready to heat and serve.

Game day…throw the foil wrapped burritos on a hot grill and roll them around until heated throughout. It's that easy !!!

34 *Tourlou, Tourlou*
(Mediterranean style roasted vegetables)

Ingredients

1 lb. green beans, trimmed and halved

1 large russet potato, peeled and cut into bit sized pieces

1 large sweet potato, peeled and cut into bite sized pieces

2 zucchinis, halved longwise and sliced

3 or 4 celery stalks, sliced into bite sized pieces

1 large onion, cut into bite sized pieces

4 large garlic cloves, chopped

1 – 28 oz. can diced tomatoes with juice

Salt and pepper to taste

3 tablespoons chopped fresh dill weed (or your favorite herb)

⅔ cup chopped fresh parsley

½ cup extra virgin olive oil, divided

Directions

Preheat oven to 400°. Place all of the cut vegetables in a large bowl (NOT the dill and parsley) and toss with the diced tomatoes. Season with salt and pepper and drizzle with ¼ cup of the olive oil. Toss again and turn the mixture into a large (9 x 13) baking dish. Sprinkle the chopped fresh dill and parsley over the vegetables. Drizzle the remaining 1/4 cup olive oil over the vegetables. Cover with a lid (or foil) and bake at 400° for 1 hour (or longer), until the vegetables are cooked throughout.

*This larger than veggie life side dish will serve 10 plus.

35 | Irish Soda Bread
(You don't need the luck of the Irish to bake this yummy soda bread!!!)

Ingredients

1 cup sour cream
1 ½ cups buttermilk
4 cups flour
1 cup sugar
1 teaspoon salt
¾ teaspoon baking soda
2 teaspoons baking powder
1 stick chilled butter
2 cups raisins
2 eggs, beaten

Directions

This recipe actually begins the night before you want to bake the bread.

In a medium non-reactive bowl, combine the sour cream and the buttermilk. Cover with plastic wrap and leave out overnight in a cool spot in the kitchen.

Preheat oven to 325°. In a large bowl, combine the flour with the sugar, salt, baking soda, and baking powder. Cut the chilled butter into small pieces and using a knife and fork incorporate the butter into the flour mixture. Stir in the raisins. Stir the beaten eggs into the buttermilk mixture then combine with the flour mixture, using a wooden spoon to stir. The dough will be wet and heavy. Turn the dough into a well-greased 10 inch iron skillet or 2 greased loaf pans. Use a knife to make a cross over the bread. This is considered an Irish blessing.

Bake at 325° for 1 hour and 10 minutes. Remove from oven to a cooling rack and brush the top of the bread with a bit of softened butter.

*I was told by a young, fine Irish man that this soda bread is better than his grandmother's but he would never tell her.

36 *Skillet Corn Bread*

Ingredients

1 cup cornmeal
1 cup flour
2 teaspoons baking powder
½ teaspoon baking soda
½ teaspoon salt
1 cup buttermilk
1 extra large egg
¼ cup honey
3 teaspoons butter, melted

Directions

Preheat oven to 425 degrees. Generously grease an 8 inch iron (preferably) skillet and set aside.

In a medium bowl combine the cornmeal with the flour, baking powder, baking soda and salt.

In a small bowl whisk the buttermilk with the egg and the honey. Pour over the dry mixture and stir to combine. Stir in the melted butter then pour the batter into the greased skillet.

Bake at 425 degrees for about 25 minutes, until golden brown on the edges and on top.

Carefully remove from oven, cut into wedges and serve with softened butter, honey or even maple syrup.

*This from scratch corn bread has become a staple in my kitchen.

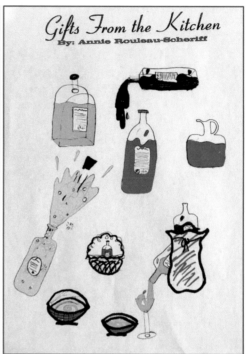

TO LONG ISLAND AND BACK... WITH LOVE

Anyone who knows me knows that Long Island is my second home. After short stints in Brooklyn and Queens (New York) I spent the better part of 10 years there. I formed lifetime friendships there (Shout out to Butcher, Sopp-Tsang, Love, Hunter-Labo & Breidenbach) Lucky me, I have been able to visit often and help my pal Amy at her summer clam bar, Crabby Amy's.

That's how I met Kevin the "clammer". I used to get clams from him, hop on a plane back to Michigan and serve up the freshest clams in the state. It has become a regular thing. Just 2 recipes in this chapter but the memories are triple digits.

37 Long Island Baked Clams

Ingredients

3 dozen little neck or top neck clams
A piece of cheese cloth
2 tablespoons olive oil
4 oz. finely chopped pancetta
⅔ cup panko bread crumbs
⅓ cup grated Parmesan cheese
½ teaspoon dried oregano
Pinch of black pepper
½ cup white wine

*Transporting fresh clams from Long Island N.Y. to Michigan has become a regular part of my travel itinerary.

Directions

Scrub the clams well under cold water. Bring about 2 inches of water in a large pot to a boil. Add all of the clams and cover the pot. Wait 7 to 8 minutes than check to see if any of the clams have started to open. You want to pluck the clams from the pot as soon as they open, carefully, with a large spoon. If some of the clams haven't opened just be patient, they will. When the steamed clams are cool enough to handle, pull off the top half of each shell, leaving the clams nestled in the bottom half of the shell. Place the clams in a shallow bake dish, side by side. Pour the cooking liquid through the cheese cloth, then drizzle a bit of the liquid over the clams to keep them from drying out. This will add a natural salt flavor to the clams.

In a medium skillet or wok, heat the olive oil. Add the pancetta and cook for a few minutes, stirring often. Add the panko and cook for a few more minutes. Add the Parmesan cheese along with the oregano and black pepper. Cook for another minute or two, then remove from the heat. If the mixture seems dry, add a bit more olive oil.

Preheat the broiler to high. Spoon some of the mixture over each of the clams, filling the entire shell. Gently pack the mixture around the clams. Drizzle some white wine over the top of the clams, then place on the center rack of the oven. Broil for 5 minutes or so, just until the clams are beginning to brown. Actual cook time will vary from oven to oven. Take care not to overcook the clams.

38 *Manhattan Clam Chowder*

Ingredients

2 tablespoons olive oil
4 pieces bacon
2 cups diced carrot
2 cups diced onion
2 cups diced celery
4 garlic cloves, finely chopped
2 teaspoons dried oregano (or thyme)
10 cups water
½ cup white wine
2 – 8 oz. bottles clam juice
1 – 28 oz. can whole tomatoes (broken up) or diced tomatoes, with juice
1 lb. red skin potatoes, half peeled and cut into bite size pieces
1 lb. chopped clams
¼ cup tomato paste
Salt, pepper (or chicken base) for seasoning
Pinch of cayenne or a dash of hot sauce
1 cup chopped fresh parsley
2 dozen little neck clams, scrubbed (optional)

Directions

Heat the olive oil in a large, heavy pot and add the bacon. Cook until the bacon is just about crisp. Add the carrot, onion and celery and cook for 10 minutes or so, over medium heat. Add the garlic and cook for 5 more minutes.

Add the water, wine, clam juice and tomatoes and bring the pot to a boil. Lower to a simmer and add the potato. Simmer for another 10 minutes or so, then add the clams and the tomato paste. Taste and season with salt and pepper or chicken base. Add the cayenne or hot sauce and the fresh parsley. Simmer for another 20 minutes or so.

Drop the scrubbed clams into the pot and cook until they open. Ladle into bowls and enjoy.

*This chowder was a favorite at a place called "Cap's" where I worked in the mid-1980's.

ADOLESCENT BEHAVIOR

We all want to remember the child we once were. These three recipes are so much fun to make with a young person. And share with everyone.

39 "𝓕𝓾𝓷 𝓡𝓸𝓵𝓵𝓼" (dessert sushi)

Ingredients

1 box Fruit roll-ups
Rice "krispy" cereal
Mini marshmallows
Butter
Assorted gummy fish and worms

Directions

Unroll the fruit roll-ups onto a flat work surface. Prepare rice krispy treats according to package directions. While the mixture is still warm, pack some onto half of the fruit roll-up.

Place gummy fish or worm over the rice and roll tightly. Trim the ends and cut into 1 inch pieces.

Fun Rolls *Fun Rolls not only really look like real life sushi, they really are fun to make!

40 Granny Smith Snickers "Salad"

Ingredients

6 – full sized Snickers bars
3 to 4 Granny Smith apples
1 – 16 oz. container Cool Whip, thawed

Directions

Cut each of the Snickers bars into 3 logs lengthwise, then into small bite sized pieces. Place in a large bowl, setting aside a few pieces for garnish.

Core the apples and cut into small bite sized pieces. (The apple bite size should be uniform with the Snickers bite.) Add to the bowl with the Snickers bites. Set aside a few pieces for garnish.

Add the Cool Whip, a bit at a time, folding everything together with a rubber spatula. Turn the mixture into a fancy serving bowl and garnish the top with the Snickers and apple pieces that were set aside.

Store covered in the refrigerator until ready to serve.

*The caramel, chocolate and peanuts from the snickers bar pairs perfectly with the tartness of the Granny Smith apple. And who doesn't like Cool Whip!

41 Hamburger Cookies

Ingredients

1 can vanilla frosting
Red, yellow and green food
coloring
1 box vanilla wafer cookies
("burger bun")
1 package Keebler Grasshopper
cookies ("burger")
1 – 6 oz. can Better Made potato
sticks ("fries")
raspberry or strawberry jam
("ketchup") for garnish (optional)
Egg wash and sesame seeds
(optional)

Directions

Spoon a heaping ½ cup of frosting into 2 small bowls. Following package directions add drops of food coloring to make green ("lettuce") frosting. Repeat with the other bowl adding drops of food coloring to make orange ("cheese").

Smear a bit of green frosting on the flat side of a vanilla wafer and a smear of orange on another to assemble the cheeseburgers. Place a Grasshopper cookie in between the two frosted wafers and gently squeeze together. A touch of frosting should come out to the edge of the wafer, identifying the lettuce and the cheese. Repeat with remaining cookies and frosting. I make the cookies in an assembly line with my nieces and nephews. They love me for it.

Scatter the potato sticks on a serving platter and place the cheeseburger cookies on top. A little dollop of red jam on the side will serve as ketchup for dipping the fries.

*Color shredded sweet coconut green for the lettuce
and secure it to the wafer with plain vanilla frosting
"mayonnaise". For "sesame seed buns", brush egg white over
each cookie and sprinkle with sesame seeds. Allow a few
minutes for the egg white to dry and secure the seeds.

*Cheeseburger sliders not only boast a super neat
presentation, they taste as good as they look!

"CHIC" CROCK-POT COOKERY

Crock Pot-Crack Pots

Crock Pot-Crack Pots

***Crock pots are NOT miracle workers. You must strategically place flavorful ingredients IN the crock pot in order for a truly tasty entrée to come OUT of the crock pot.

***While crock pots have their place at social settings they are not welcome at formal events. Use them to prepare the food but always transfer to an attractive serving vessel.

***If you're going to be away from the kitchen for extended periods of time (7 hours or more) always choose the "low" setting on your crock pot.

***If your sleep pattern is 7 to 9 hours it's the perfect time to plug in the cooker and have dreamy dreams about yummy food. Only it won't be a dream.

***Remember that not only does the crock pot save you time but also $$$$ as the crock can turn cheap meat into first class pigs ass !!!

42   *Ratatouille* (plus oven method)

Ingredients

1 – 1 lb. eggplant, peeled and cut into 1 inch chunks
1 ½ teaspoons salt, divided
1 large onion, cut in half lengthwise and thinly sliced
1 each large green and red pepper, cut into strips
1 lb. zucchini, sliced
1 ½ lbs. Roma tomatoes, halved and cut into wedges
3 tablespoons tomato paste
3 tablespoons extra-virgin olive oil
1 tablespoon sugar
¼ teaspoon black pepper
3 large garlic cloves, minced
½ cup chopped fresh basil
¼ cup capers, drained

Directions

Place the eggplant in a colander over the sink and toss with ¼ teaspoon of the salt. Let stand for 30 minutes. Meanwhile, prep all of the other veggies. Whisk together the tomato paste with the olive oil, sugar, pepper, garlic and remaining 1 ¼ teaspoons salt in a small bowl.

Layer half each of the onions, followed by the eggplant, pepper strips, zucchini, and tomatoes in a large greased crock pot. Spoon half of the tomato paste mixture over the veggies and repeat with another layer beginning with the onions and ending with the remaining tomato paste mixture. Cover and cook on low for 8 to 9 hours or until all of the vegetables are tender throughout. Stir in the basil and the capers and serve hot, warm or room temperature over crostini (toasted bread rounds,) with crackers or as a side car to meat off the grill.

*Calling all Vegetarians and Vegans!!!! Oven method:
Bake covered at 300° for 3 hours.*

43 Pulled Mexican Chicken

Ingredients

4 to 6 boneless, skinless chicken breasts, 3 – 3 ½ lbs.
2 packages taco seasoning
1 large jar salsa (about 3 cups)
1 – 4 oz. can chopped green chilies
1 sweet bell pepper, chopped
1 large onion, chopped
1 – 4 oz. can sliced black olives (optional)

Directions

Place the chicken breasts in a medium to large greased crock pot. Top with the taco seasoning followed by all of the other ingredients. Cover and cook on low for 6 to 8 hours. Use forks to pull the chicken into shreds. Enjoy the spicy chicken meat in tacos, burritos, or to serve over rice.

*You'll create your own ideas for this simple but super flavorful crock full of south of the border goodness.

Chicken Enchilada Pie

Ingredients

2 cups prepared pulled Mexican chicken
1 – 15oz. can pinto beans, drained
2 cups shredded sharp cheddar cheese, divided
8 soft corn tortillas
½ cup prepared enchilada sauce (red or green)
½ cup chopped fresh cilantro

Directions

In a large bowl, combine the chicken with the beans and 1 ½ cups of the cheese. Arrange 4 of the corn tortillas in the bottom of a greased pie plate. (Cut the tortillas in half for a better fit around the pie plate.) Fill with the chicken-bean mixture and top with the other tortillas. Scatter a bit of cheese over the tortillas. Ladle the enchilada sauce on top of the tortillas. Scatter the remaining cheese over the sauce and top with the chopped cilantro. Bake at 350° for 30 minutes, until the pie is heated throughout and the top is golden brown. Slice into wedges and serve.

44 *Crock Pot Roast "A la Annie"*

Ingredients

1 – 3 to 3 ½ lb. chunk pot roast
2 to 3 tablespoons olive oil
Salt and pepper
8 to 10 garlic cloves, peeled, smashed and halved
1 – 15 oz. can crushed tomatoes
½ cup full bodied red wine
3 tablespoons instant tapioca
1 teaspoon Worcestershire sauce
Additional salt and pepper to taste

Directions

Heat a large no-stick grill pan (or large skillet) over medium-high heat. Rub the meat with the olive oil and generously season both sides of the meat with salt and pepper. Place the meat in the hot skillet and sear for 7 to 10 minutes depending on how thick the cut is. Flip the meat and sear on the other side. Look for a deep sear that is dark in color.

Transfer the seared meat to a large, greased crock pot. Arrange the garlic around the meat.

In a small bowl, whisk together the crushed tomato with the red wine, tapioca and Worcestershire sauce. Pour the mixture over the meat. Slow cook for 4 hours on high or 6 hours on low. Taste the sauce after cooking to see if additional seasoning is needed.

*Your house will be filled with a yummy fragrance that will have your family running to the dinner table.

45 French Stew (plus oven method)

Ingredients

3 to 4 carrots, sliced
5 celery ribs, sliced
2 large onions, chopped
4 to 5 potatoes, peeled and cut into bite size pieces
2 lbs. stew meat, cut into bite size pieces
2 ¼ cups tomato juice
7 tablespoons instant tapioca
2 ½ tablespoons sugar
1 teaspoon each salt and pepper

Directions

Crock-Pot Method:

Layer the carrots in the bottom of a large, greased crock pot. Follow with the celery, onions and potatoes. Toss the stew meat in a bit of olive oil, salt and pepper and arrange it over the potatoes.

In a small bowl, whisk together the tomato juice with the tapioca, sugar, salt and pepper. Pour the mixture evenly over the meat. Cover and cook on low for 6 to 8 hours. Do not stir until ready to serve.

Oven Method:

Preheat oven to 400°. Grease a 3 quart Dutch oven and arrange the prepared stew meat in the bottom of the pot followed by the celery, carrots, potatoes and, lastly, the onions.

Pour the tomato mixture over the onions. Cover and place in a 400° oven for 30 minutes. Lower the oven temperature to 300° and continue to cook covered for another 3 hours or so. Don't stir the stew until you are ready to serve it.

*Words can't describe the aroma that will fill your home, no matter the method you choose.

46 Awesome Kielbasa and Sauerkraut

Ingredients

2 lbs. fresh sauerkraut, drained
1 ½ cups apple sauce
1 package dried onion soup mix
1 bottle (or can) robust beer
2 to 3 cups water
2 lbs. Dearborn smoked kielbasa,
cut into 2 inch pieces

Directions

In a large crock-pot, combine the sauerkraut with the apple sauce, onion soup mix and the beer. Add just enough water to cover the kraut. Stir well. Add the kielbasa and cover. Cook on high for 3 hours or low for 5 hours.

Serve with mashed potatoes or crusty bread. This is a great half time choice for any sporting event.

BRUNCH!

Deviled eggs, quiche, French toast, sausage and coffee cake. This chapter offers a complete brunch menu that will serve 12 and have a little something for everyone.

You can make (or prep) each selection in advance, giving you back valuable time needed to play hostess. And brew the coffee.

47 Sweet and Sour Deviled Eggs

Ingredients

12 hard cooked eggs, peeled and chilled
5 teaspoons sugar
5 teaspoons apple cider vinegar
1 teaspoon salt
1 teaspoon prepared (yellow) mustard
¼ cup mayonnaise (not miracle whip)
paprika and dried parsley for garnish

Directions

Begin by cooking the eggs. Place the eggs in a heavy pot and fill with water to completely cover the eggs with an inch of water. Bring the pot to a boil. Turn off the heat, cover and set the timer for 8 minutes. (a bit longer if the eggs are jumbo) Quickly remove the eggs and submerge them in a bowl of iced water.

Peel the eggs, cut them in half length wise and pop out the yolks into a small bowl. Carefully wrap the egg whites and store in the refrigerator until ready to fill.

Use a potato masher to smash the yolks. Dissolve the sugar into apple cider vinegar then stir it into the mashed yolks along with the salt, mustard and mayonnaise. Stir well to incorporate all of the ingredients. Lightly season the egg white halves with black pepper. Spoon a heaping teaspoon of the yolk filling into each of the egg white halves. Arrange the eggs on a holiday serving plate and sprinkle with paprika and dried parsley flakes.

You can prepare the yummy yolk filling a day in advance but don't stuff the egg whites until just before serving. Store the egg white "shells" covered with a damp paper towel and wrapped in plastic to keep from drying out.

48 Blueberry Boy Bait

Ingredients

2 cups flour
1 cup sugar
2 teaspoons baking powder
¼ teaspoon salt
²/₃ cup vegetable oil
1 cup milk (preferable whole or 2%)
2 large eggs
3 cups fresh blueberries, washed

Topping:
3 tablespoons sugar
1 teaspoon cinnamon

Directions

Preheat oven to 350 degrees.

In a large bowl combine the flour with the sugar, baking powder, and salt. Use a fork to sift the ingredients together.

Add the vegetable oil, milk and eggs and beat with an electric mixer for 3 minutes, scraping down the sides of the bowl.

Pour the batter into a greased 9 X 13 (or similar) baking dish. Scatter the blueberries over the batter, as evenly as possible.

Combine the 3 remaining tablespoons of sugar with the cinnamon and sprinkle over the blueberries.

Bake at 350 degrees for about 50 minutes, until baked throughout and golden on the top and the edges.

*I fell in love with this recipe during blueberry season. This not too sweet cake serves well anytime.

49 Crust-Less Quiche with Bacon, Onion and Arugula

Ingredients

½ lb. bacon, cooked and chopped (5 to 6 slices)
1 large onion, chopped
1 tablespoon olive oil
3 ½ oz. arugula (half of a 7 oz. bag)
1 ½ cups shredded Mexican blend cheese
3 large eggs
1 – 16 oz. container egg whites, egg beaters, or 5 or more additional eggs
¼ cup milk, half and half, or cream
Salt and pepper to taste

Directions

Heat the olive oil in a small skillet and sauté the onion until tender and beginning to brown. Transfer to a medium bowl. In the same skillet, wilt the arugula, adding a spritz of water to prevent it from scorching. As soon as the arugula is wilted, tip it into the bowl with the onion. Add the chopped bacon and toss. Add the shredded cheese and toss.

Preheat oven to 350°.

In a separate bowl, whisk together the egg substitute with the eggs and the milk. Pour over the bacon, onion, and arugula mixture and gently stir to combine. Season lightly with salt and pepper. Remember there is salt in the bacon and the cheese. Pour the quiche filling into an 8 or 9 inch pie or quiche pan. Sprinkle with a bit of fresh or dried parsley.

Bake the quiche at 350° for 50 minutes or until set throughout and beginning to brown around the edges. Remove from oven and cut into wedges. Serve hot.

*The peppery bite from the arugula lends a kick to this flavorful egg dish. You're not breaking any rules if you bake it in a crust.

50 Oven Baked French Toast

Ingredients

1 – 1 lb. loaf French or Italian bread, cut 2 inches thick on the diagonal
8 eggs
2 cups milk
1 ½ cups half and half
2 teaspoons vanilla
1 teaspoon cinnamon
¾ cup butter (1 ½ sticks)
1 ½ cups brown sugar
3 tablespoons light corn syrup

Directions

Grease a 9 x 13 (or similar sized deep pan) and arrange the bread slices on the bottom, side by side but not overlapping. Beat together the eggs with the milk, half and half, vanilla and the cinnamon. Pour the mixture over the bread slices, cover and refrigerate overnight. There is a lot of egg mixture so be sure to utilize every inch of the baking dish with bread!

The next morning, preheat the oven to 350° . In a small saucepan over low heat combine the butter, brown sugar and corn syrup. Cook until the mixture is well combined and just begins to bubble, stirring often. Pour the syrup evenly over the top of the soaked bread slices. Bake at 350° for 40 minutes or so, until golden brown.

*Serve hot with a side of your favorite breakfast meat (my choice, turkey sausage.)

A sprinkle of powdered sugar rounds out a special occasion presentation.

51 *Mustard Marmalade Sausages*

Ingredients

12 breakfast sausage patties
(pork or turkey)
OR
14 breakfast sausage links (pork
or turkey)
2/3 cup orange marmalade
1/3 cup whole grain mustard
Fresh rosemary leaves (optional)

Directions

Cook the sausage in a large (no-stick) skillet over medium heat until brown. Remove from skillet and discard any grease if necessary. Return the skillet to a medium-low heat and add the orange marmalade. As the marmalade melts, stir in the mustard and blend well. Return the sausage to the skillet and toss with the sauce until heated throughout. Sprinkle with a touch of fresh rosemary leaves just before serving.

THE LAST

It was twenty years (almost to the day) when budget cuts at the paper forced my recipe column to retire.

These over the top decedent dessert bites seemed to be the perfect send off.

52 Death by Chocolate

Prepare a box of chocolate pudding, then refrigerate until serving

Ingredients

For the brownies:
1 stick butter
2 oz. unsweetened chocolate
1 cup sugar
2 eggs
1 teaspoon vanilla
1 cup flour

For the ganache
1 cup heavy cream
1 cup dark chocolate chips, plus more

Directions

Preheat oven to 350°. Melt the butter along with the chocolate in a medium sauce pan over low heat. Remove from heat, then stir in the sugar, followed by the eggs (one at a time,) the vanilla and, lastly, the flour. Stir well, then turn the batter into a square 8 x 8 greased baking pan. Bake at 350° for 30 minutes or so, until the brownies are cooked throughout. Don't overcook the brownies.

For the ganache

Heat 1 cup of heavy cream in a small sauce pan over low heat. When the cream begins to steam, stir in a cup of dark chocolate chips. Add heat. Add more chips until the mixture resembles a thick sauce consistency. Set aside.

To assemble the bites, cut the brownies into 1 inch square pieces. Place a heaping teaspoon of the chocolate pudding in the center of a Chinese serving spoon. Top with a piece of the brownie. Drizzle a heaping teaspoon of the warm ganache over the brownie. Repeat with remaining pudding, brownies and ganache to create up to 32 over the top chocolate one (or maybe two) bite wonders.

Death by chocolate bites can be served warm, if you time it right, or cooled. Super yummy either way for sure!

In 1996 I started writing a "food column" in the Grosse Pointe News. I like to think that I was a sort of recipe whisperer. Combing through countless cook books and food magazines (thanks to my gal pal Bonnie) searching for great recipes to pass along to the community and my readers.

Many recipes never made the cut and I often added my own touches to many. As the years moved along there were recipes that I fell in love with and found myself making them again and again. Some of them so often that I no longer needed a recipe.

Friday was my deadline day each week. Having never been a great student, at times my freelance job seemed more like a homework assignment. I am grateful to have had many friends, family and readers who brought me wonderful recipes to share. Many that you'll find in this cookbook.

I chose "52 Reasons" as the title of my cookbook to represent the number of recipes that I submitted to the newspaper each year. It is my hope that these recipes (that I cherish) will give you a reason to step into your kitchen and find the joy that I do, when cooking.

Nothing makes me happier than feeding my family and friends. Anyone who knows me knows just how true that is. When you come to my house, you will be fed. That is a given.

A la Annie continued for 20 years, almost to the day.

Printed in the United States
By Bookmasters